Evan Hause

Little Suite for Piano
"The Seasons"

ISBN 978-1-4234-8940-5

EDWARD B. MARKS MUSIC COMPANY / **EXCLUSIVELY DISTRIBUTED BY** HAL•LEONARD® CORPORATION

7777 W. BLUEMOUND RD. P.O. BOX 13819 MILWAUKEE, WI 53213

www.ebmarks.com
www.halleonard.com

CONTENTS

Little Suite for Piano
"The Seasons"

I Lake Reflections (Summer)

EVAN HAUSE

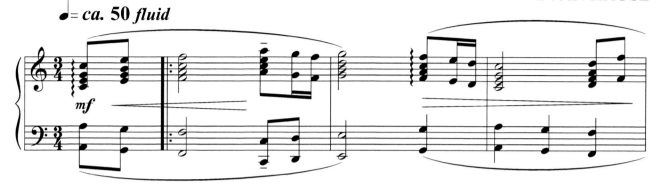

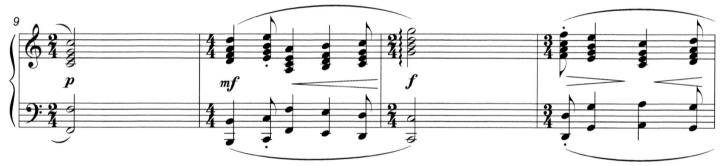

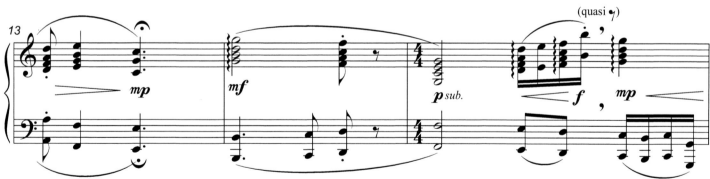

II Melancholy Waltz (Fall)

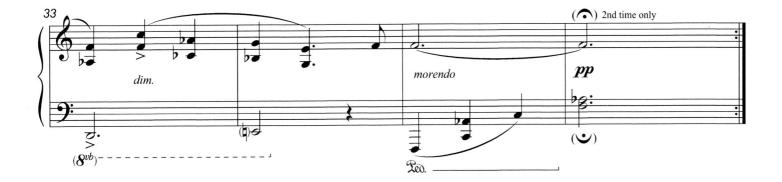

III Frozen Sunset (Winter)

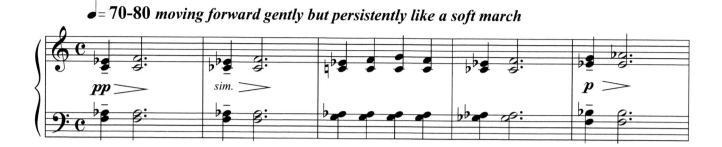

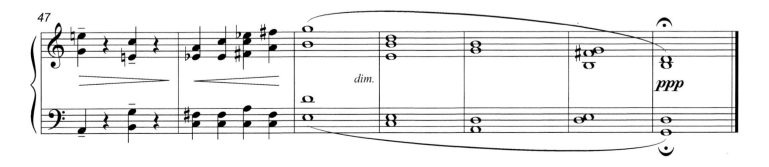

IV Wedding Music (Spring)

♩= *ca.* **116 Slowly lilting;** *dolce*

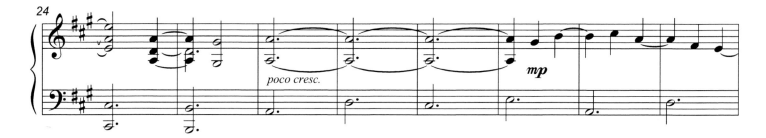

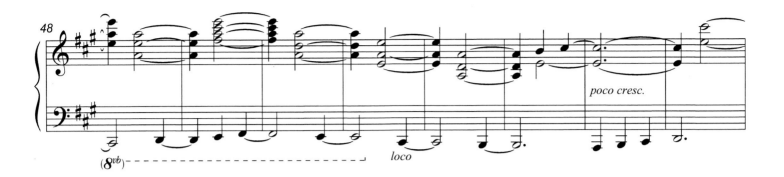